SUPER SIMPLE BODY

INSIDE THE BLOOD

KARIN HALVORSON, M.D.
Consulting Editor, Diane Craig, M.A./Reading Specialist

Super Sandcastle

An Imprint of Abdo Publishing
abdopublishing.com

VISIT US AT ABDOPUBLISHING.COM

Published by Abdo Publishing, a division of ABDO, PO Box 398166, Minneapolis, Minnesota 55439. Copyright © 2016 by Abdo Consulting Group, Inc. International copyrights reserved in all countries. No part of this book may be reproduced in any form without written permission from the publisher. Super SandCastle™ is a trademark and logo of Abdo Publishing.

Printed in the United States of America,
North Mankato, Minnesota
102015
012016

Editor: Liz Salzmann
Content Developer: Nancy Tuminelly
Cover and Interior Design: Mighty Media, Inc.
Photo Credits: Shutterstock

Library of Congress Cataloging-in-Publication Data
Halvorson, Karin, 1979- author.
  Inside the blood / Karin Halvorson, M.D. ; consulting editor, Diane Craig, M.A./reading specialist.
     pages cm. -- (Super simple body)
  ISBN 978-1-62403-941-6
1. Blood--Juvenile literature. 2. Blood--Circulation--Juvenile literature. I. Title. II. Series: Halvorson, Karin, 1979- Super simple body.
  QP91.H24 2016
  612.1'1--dc23
                    2015020587

Super SandCastle™ books are created by a team of professional educators, reading specialists, and content developers around five essential components—phonemic awareness, phonics, vocabulary, text comprehension, and fluency—to assist young readers as they develop reading skills and strategies and increase their general knowledge. All books are written, reviewed, and leveled for guided reading and early reading intervention programs for use in shared, guided, and independent reading and writing activities to support a balanced approach to literacy instruction.

NOTE TO ADULTS

THIS BOOK is all about encouraging children to learn the science of how their bodies work! Be there to help make science fun and interesting for young readers. Many activities are included in this book to help children further explore what they've learned. Some require adult assistance and/ or permission. Make sure children have appropriate places where they can do the activities safely.

Children may also have questions about what they've learned. Offer help and guidance when they have questions. Most of all, encourage them to keep exploring and learning new things!

CONTENTS

YOUR BODY 4

ALL ABOUT BLOOD 6

RED BLOOD CELLS 8

WHITE BLOOD CELLS 10

PLATELETS 12

PLASMA SOUP 14

BLOOD VESSELS 16

BLOOD PUMPERS 18

BLOOD TYPES 20

BLOOD TRANSFERS 22

BLOOD-TYPE HYPE 24

STEM CELLS 26

WHAT'S A BRUISE? 28

THE COLOR OF BLOOD 30

BLOOD SUCKERS 31

GLOSSARY 32

YOUR BODY

YOUR BLOOD

You're amazing! So is your body!

Your body has a lot of different parts. Your **kidneys**, skin, blood, muscles, and bones all work together every day. They keep you moving. Even when you don't realize it.

Blood is an important part of you. It brings oxygen and fuel to your whole body!

You've probably seen blood before. It comes out when you get a cut.

You can feel blood pumping through your body. It's called your pulse!

HAVE YOU EVER HAD A CUT?

ALL ABOUT
BLOOD

Blood passes through your heart. Your heart pumps the blood. Each pump brings blood to different parts of your body. Blood vessels carry the blood.

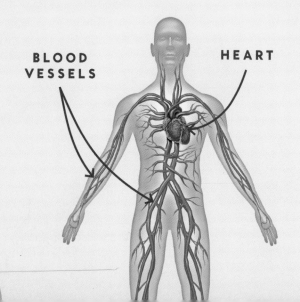

BLOOD
VESSELS

HEART

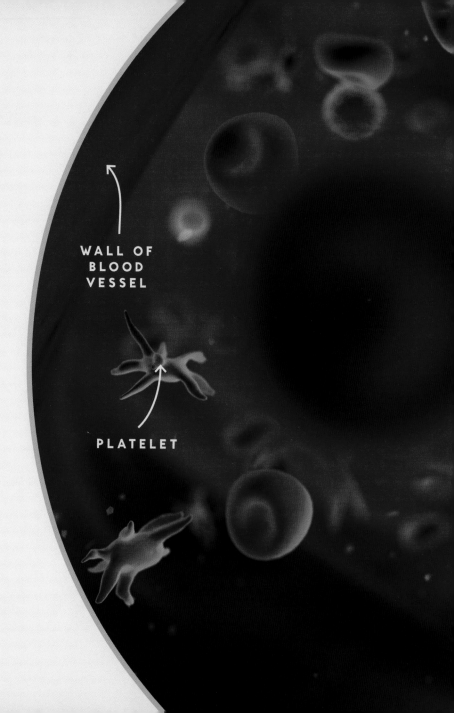

WALL OF
BLOOD
VESSEL

PLATELET

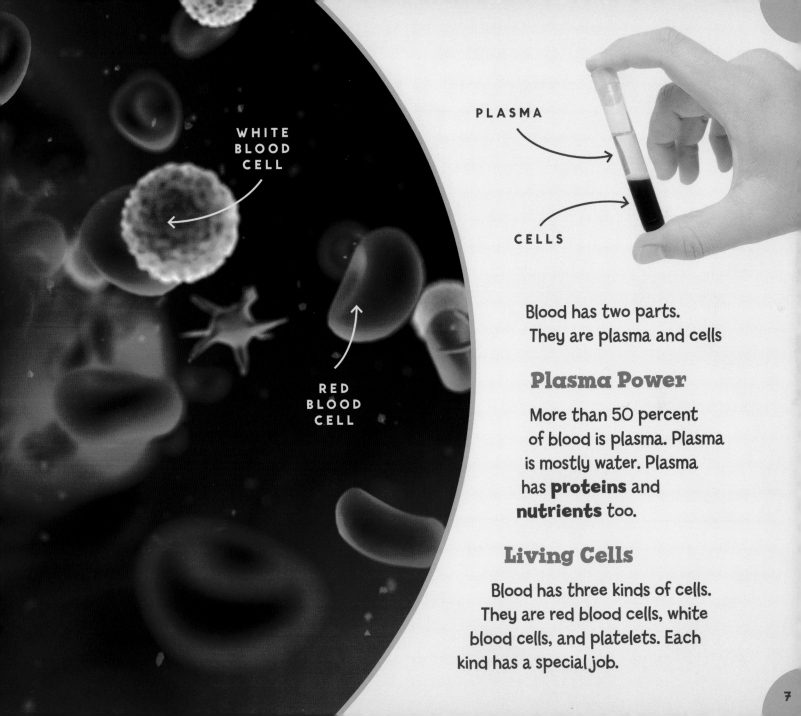

WHITE
BLOOD
CELL

RED
BLOOD
CELL

PLASMA

CELLS

Blood has two parts.
They are plasma and cells

Plasma Power

More than 50 percent
of blood is plasma. Plasma
is mostly water. Plasma
has **proteins** and
nutrients too.

Living Cells

Blood has three kinds of cells.
They are red blood cells, white
blood cells, and platelets. Each
kind has a special job.

RED
BLOOD CELLS

Your body needs oxygen. It keeps your organs working. Red blood cells carry oxygen all over your body.

RED BLOOD CELLS SEEN
THROUGH A MICROSCOPE

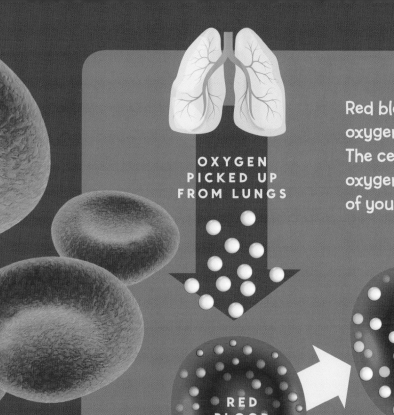

OXYGEN PICKED UP FROM LUNGS

Red blood cells pick up oxygen in your lungs. The cells drop off oxygen in other parts of your body.

RED BLOOD CELL

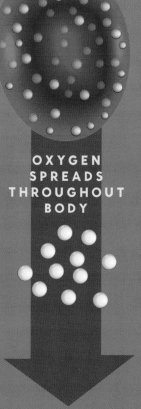

OXYGEN SPREADS THROUGHOUT BODY

OXYGEN BINDS WITH HEMOGLOBIN

HEMOGLOBIN

Red blood cells have a special **protein**. It is called hemoglobin (*HEE-muh-gloh-bin*). It has iron in it. Hemoglobin holds the oxygen.

WHITE
BLOOD CELLS

White blood cells keep you healthy. When you are sick, your body makes white blood cells.

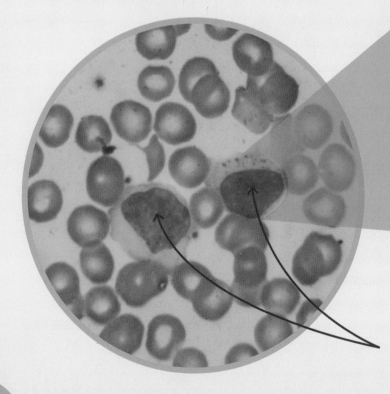

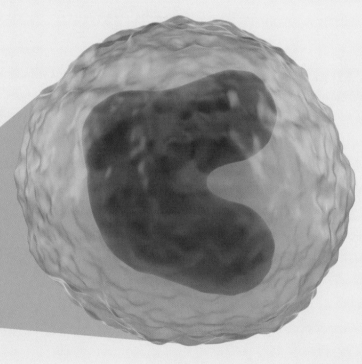

WHITE BLOOD CELLS SEEN THROUGH A MICROSCOPE

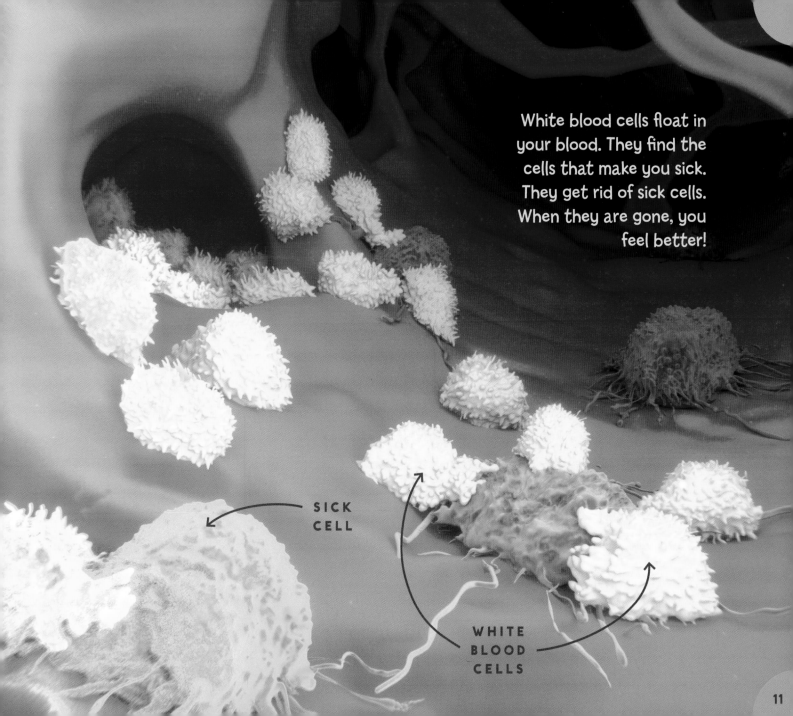

White blood cells float in your blood. They find the cells that make you sick. They get rid of sick cells. When they are gone, you feel better!

SICK CELL

WHITE BLOOD CELLS

PLATELETS

P latelets are a kind of blood cell. They help when you have a cut.

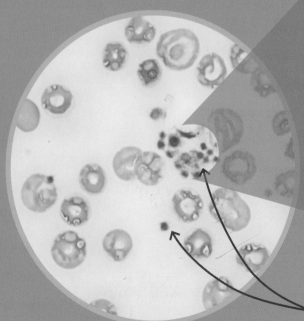

PLATELETS SEEN
THROUGH A MICROSCOPE

When skin is cut, blood comes out. Platelets surround the cut. They stick to the edges of the cut. They make a blood clot. The clot covers the cut.

That is how a scab is made. The cut heals under the scab. Then the scab falls off.

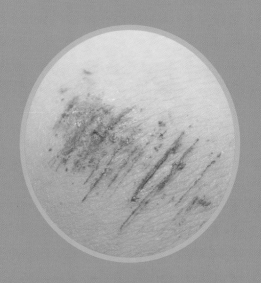

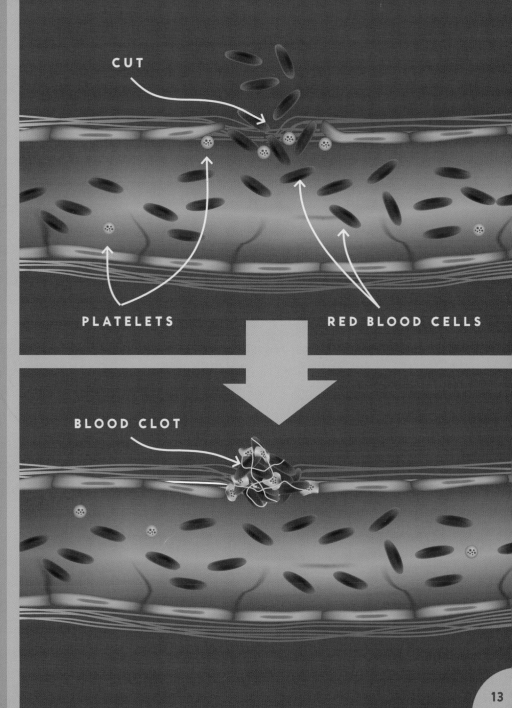

CUT

PLATELETS

RED BLOOD CELLS

BLOOD CLOT

PLASMA SOUP

WHAT IS BLOOD MADE OF?

WHAT YOU NEED: MEASURING CUP, 2 CUPS CORN SYRUP, LARGE DRINKING GLASS, MEASURING SPOONS, 6 TEASPOONS COLORED BALL SPRINKLES, 1 CUP RED CANDIES, 4 MINI MARSHMALLOWS, LARGE SPOON

HOW TO DO IT

1. Pour the syrup in the glass.

2. Add the sprinkles.

3. Add the red candies.

4. Add the marshmallows.

5. Stir the ingredients together.

WHAT'S HAPPENING?

The syrup is the water in plasma. The red candies are the red blood cells. The marshmallows are the white blood cells. The sprinkles are the platelets.

BLOOD
VESSELS

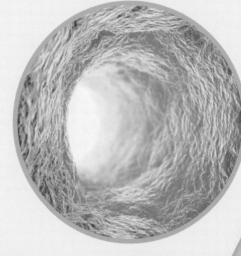

Blood vessels carry blood all over the body. There are two kinds of blood vessels. They are arteries and veins. Arteries carry blood away from the heart. Veins carry blood to the heart.

INSIDE A BLOOD VESSEL

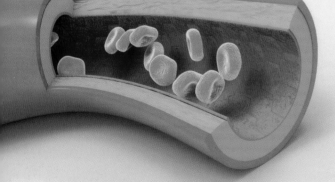

VEINS

ARTERIES

Clean Blood

The **pulmonary** vein takes clean blood from the lungs to the heart. The heart pumps blood out through the arteries. The arteries take the blood all over the body. Your body gets energy from the blood.

Used Blood

Then the used blood goes back to the heart through veins. The pulmonary artery takes the used blood from the heart to the lungs. The lungs clean the blood.

Then it starts all over again!

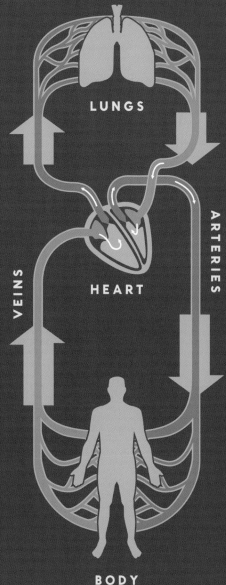

LUNGS

ARTERIES

VEINS

HEART

BODY

BLOOD PUMPERS

FEEL YOUR BLOOD MOVING!

WHAT YOU NEED: CLAY, TOOTHPICK, STOPWATCH, NOTEBOOK, PEN

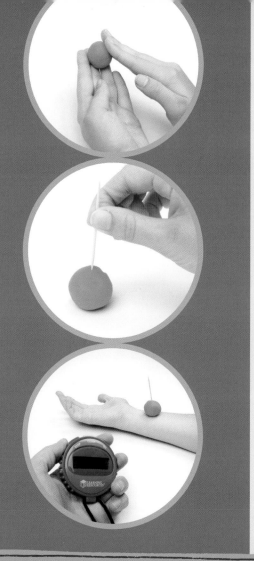

HOW TO DO IT

1. Make a ball of clay the size of a quarter.

2. Stick a toothpick into the clay.

3. Hold your arm out with your **palm** facing up. Put the clay on your wrist with the toothpick sticking up.

4. Watch the toothpick. It should move every few seconds. Count how many times it moves in 1 minute. Write down the number.

5. Do jumping jacks or run for 3 minutes. Put the clay back on your wrist. Count how many times the toothpick moves in 1 minute.

WHAT'S HAPPENING?

Each time your heart pumps blood, the toothpick moves. Blood brings energy to your body. When you exercise, you use more energy. Your heart pumps blood faster.

BLOOD
TYPES

People have different kinds of blood. There are four groups of blood. They are A, B, AB, and O.

Some people have a special **protein** in their blood. Blood with the special protein is positive. Blood without the protein is negative.

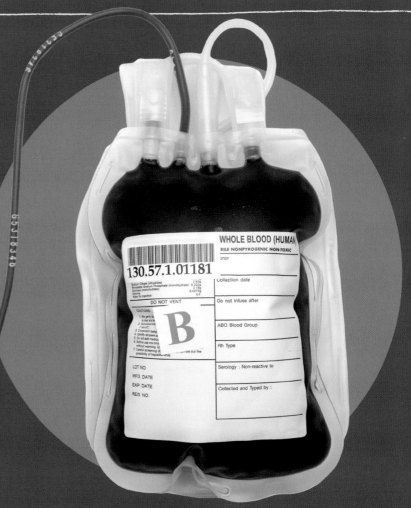

You get your blood type from your parents.

There are eight blood types.

A POSITIVE

A NEGATIVE

B POSITIVE

B NEGATIVE

AB POSITIVE

AB NEGATIVE

O POSITIVE

O NEGATIVE

{ FAST FACT }

Dogs have four blood types. Cats have 11. Cows have 800!

BLOOD
TRANSFERS

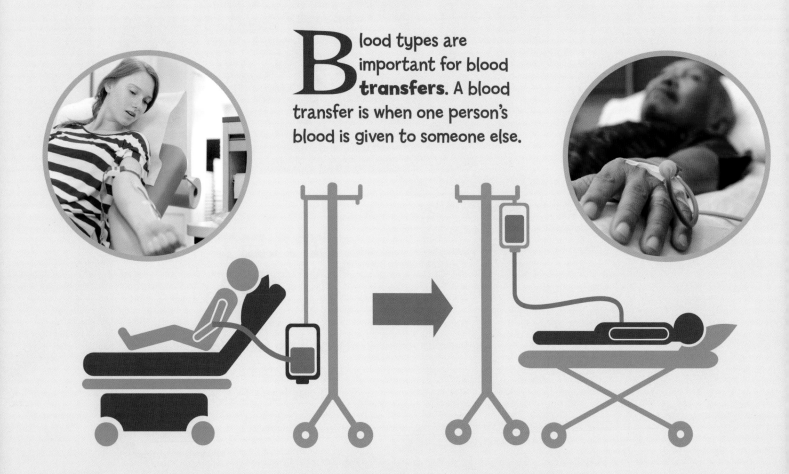

Blood types are important for blood **transfers**. A blood transfer is when one person's blood is given to someone else.

People need new blood for many reasons. People may lose blood in accidents. Some people have bodies that don't make healthy blood.

Only some blood types can be shared. If the wrong type is used, the person getting the blood gets sick.

IF YOUR BLOOD TYPE IS ...	YOU CAN RECEIVE ...							
	O-	O+	B-	B+	A-	A+	AB-	AB+
O-	YES	NO	NO	NO	NO	NO	NO	NO
O+	YES	YES	NO	NO	NO	NO	NO	NO
B-	YES	NO	YES	NO	NO	NO	NO	NO
B+	YES	YES	YES	YES	NO	NO	NO	NO
A-	YES	NO	NO	NO	YES	NO	NO	NO
A+	YES	YES	NO	NO	YES	YES	NO	NO
AB-	YES	NO	YES	NO	YES	NO	YES	NO
AB+	YES	YES	YES	YES	YES	YES	YES	YES

BLOOD-TYPE HYPE

BLOOD TYPE IS IMPORTANT!

WHAT YOU NEED: 5 CLEAR PLASTIC GLASSES, PERMANENT MARKER, MILK, RED AND BLUE FOOD COLORING

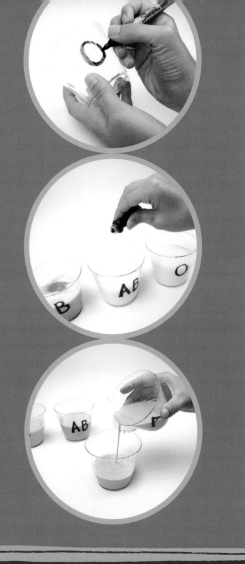

HOW TO DO IT

1. Label four glasses "O," "A," "B," and "AB."

2. Fill the labeled glasses halfway with milk.

3. Put 2 drops of red food coloring in the A glass. Put 2 drops of blue food coloring in the B glass. Put 1 drop of each color in the AB glass. Put no food coloring in the O glass.

4. Combine milk from two glasses in the empty glass. Test different combinations. In which order can you add two together so the milk poured first doesn't change color?

WHAT'S HAPPENING?

The color in each glass is a blood group. Sometimes the milk changes color when a second blood group is added. That means the second blood group can't share blood with the first blood group.

STEM CELLS

Bones make stem cells. Stem cells are special. They can turn into many different kinds of cells. They can become blood cells.

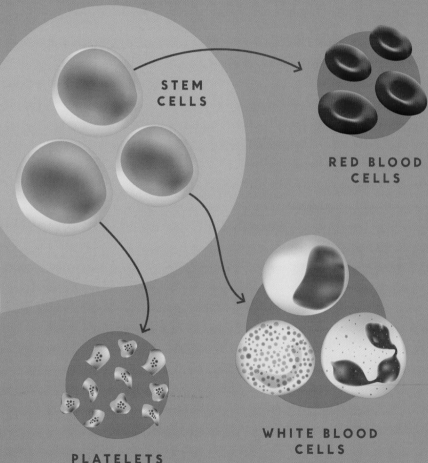

STEM CELLS

RED BLOOD CELLS

PLATELETS

WHITE BLOOD CELLS

White blood cells fight colds. When you have a cold, stem cells turn into white blood cells.

Platelets stop cuts from bleeding. When you get a cut, stem cells turn into platelets.

WHAT'S A BRUISE?

A bruise is blood under your skin. Let's say you bang your leg against something. This breaks blood vessels. Blood pools under your skin. It makes a dark blob.

White blood cells slowly eat up the blood. The blob gets lighter. The bruise goes away after a few days.

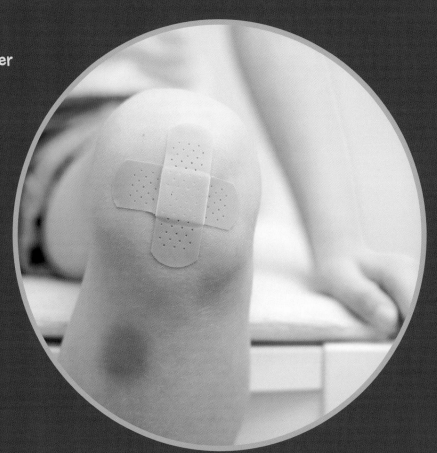

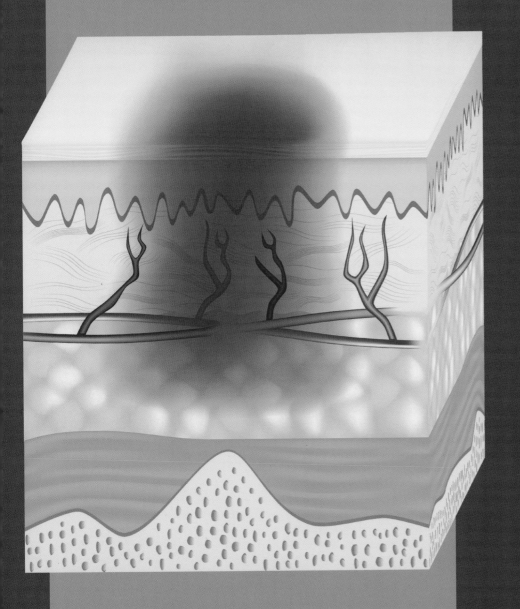

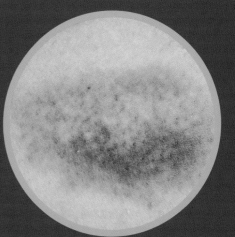

NEW BRUISE

OLD BRUISE

THE
COLOR
OF BLOOD

Everyone knows blood is red. But not all blood is the same shade of red.

Iron mixes with oxygen in your arteries. This turns blood bright red.

There is less iron in your veins. The blood there is dark red.

BLOOD
SUCKERS

Vampires are not real. But some animals do drink blood! They bite people. Watch out!

MOSQUITO

BED BUG

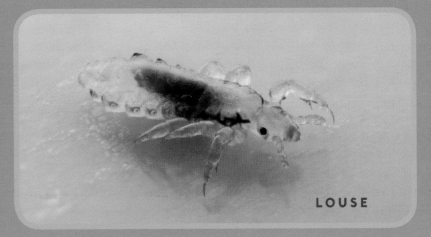

LOUSE

KIDNEY - an organ in the body that turns waste from the blood into urine.

NUTRIENT - something that helps living things grow. Vitamins, minerals, and proteins are nutrients.

PALM - the inside of your hand between your wrist and fingers.

PROTEIN - a combination of certain kinds of chemical elements. Proteins are found in all plant and animal cells.

PULMONARY - having to do with the lungs.

TRANSFER - to pass from one thing or place to another.

VAMPIRE - a made-up monster that is a dead person who drinks the blood of living people.

GLOSSARY